MW01223643

HOW TO

WITH A BLOG TOUR

"A. Terry offers a lot of practical, step-by-step advice for authors who want to increase sales and reach new readers through the tried-and-true method of virtual book tours."

- Elaine Wilkes, PhD, award-winning author, creator of "How To Get Your Book Sold To Libraries" Udemy e-course

HOW TO PROMOTE YOUR BOOK WITH A BLOG TOUR

BOOK MARKETING SURVIVAL GUIDE
V.2

A. Terry

Body and Soul Publishing
Colorado Springs, CO

Shelley Hitz
P.O. Box 6542
Colorado Springs, CO 80934
www.trainingauthors.com

Earnings Disclaimer: There is no promise or representation that you will make a certain amount of sales, or any sales, as a result of using the techniques that are outlined within this book. Any earnings, revenue, or results using these marketing strategies are strictly estimates and there is no guarantee that you will have the same results. You accept the risk that the earnings and income statements differ by individual. The use of our information, products and services should be based on your own due diligence and you agree that we are not liable for your success or failure.

Full Disclosure: Some of the links in this book may be affiliate links (excluding any and all links to Amazon) and we may earn a small commission when you make a purchase through them. By law (FTC), we must disclose this. However, we want to ensure you that we only endorse products and services we believe in and would or do use ourselves.

Book Layout ©2013 Book Design Templates
www.trainingauthors.com/booktemplates

Ordering Information:
Quantity sales. Special discounts are available on quantity purchases by corporations, associations, and others. For details, contact the "Special Sales Department" at the address above.

How to Promote Your Book with a Blog Tour / A. Terry. -- 1st ed.

Printed in the United States of America

ISBN-13: 978-0692228692
ISBN-10: 0692228691

TABLE OF CONTENTS

Before You Begin

If you are just getting started on your book marketing journey, we highly recommend reading the "Gear Up" post on our blog before you begin this book. That post will give you a good understanding of the foundation needed to successfully market your book.

Check out our four tips for beginners here:
www.trainingauthors.com/book-marketing-journey

FOREWORD

If you have already published a book, chances are you are looking for effective online marketing book strategies to help you sell your book. You have spent hours brainstorming, writing, editing, and publishing your book. Now what? Now it is time to let people know that your book exists. It does not matter if you have a great book if no one knows about it.

So, how can you gain more fans and sell more books through online marketing book strategies? I highly recommend that you consider a virtual book tour. What is a virtual book tour anyway? Basically, it is a blog tour where you share guest posts on different blogs to promote you, your blog, your products, and your books.

When A. Terry approached me about publishing this book on blog tours, I knew it would be helpful to many authors. Not only does she provide step-by-step instructions on how to set up your blog tour, she is sharing a book marketing method that actually works. Myself, A. Terry, and many other authors have found success using blog tours to promote our books.

The Top 3 Reasons Why Should You Consider Guest Blogging

1) **It is free.** Who doesn't want free book marketing, right? However, you do have to spend your time researching and writing the posts, but you don't have to pay for the advertising you will get from these posts.

2) **It is forever.** Your guest post will remain on that blog forever to promote you, your products and your books.

3) **It is fun.** Not only do you get tons of increased blog traffic, exposure, new fans, and new customers; but you also meet some amazing people in your field of expertise. I have found it fun to network and get to know other key players in my niche.

A Few Tips to an Effective Guest Blogging Tour

If you are going to invest the time into scheduling a guest blogging tour and writing the posts, you'll want to make the most out of this online marketing book idea.

Here are three tips:

1) **Do your research**. Your tour will be much more effective if you choose high traffic, popular blogs. You know that a blog is popular by finding out their Google page rank and Alexa ranking. In the beginning, you may still want to target a few smaller blogs, but don't be afraid to approach the authority blogs in your niche!

2) **Provide high quality content**. Be a great guest and provide unique, high quality content for your host. Make yourself stand out by putting your best foot forward.

3) **Develop a plan**. You will need to plan how long your tour will be and develop a schedule for your tour. If you are doing a longer tour, you will need tools to help you stay organized. Use what works best for you whether it's an Excel spreadsheet, a Word document or pen and paper.

-Shelley Hitz
Best-selling author and owner of TrainingAuthors.com

A Gift for You...

Before you dig in to the information in this book,
we want to give you our training,
"Building a Book Marketing Plan,"
a $27 value, free of charge.

Why?

Simply because we enjoy helping authors succeed.

In this training, you will download
our master book marketing plan template
with a PDF training report.

Claim your free copy at the link below:
www.trainingauthors.com/freegift

PART ONE

Blog Tour Basics

CHAPTER ONE

Introduction to Blog Tours

So you wrote a book. Congratulations! But you didn't stop there. You edited it and re-edited it, only to go back and find more sections to edit all over again. You probably ran it by some beta readers or copyeditors for feedback. After that, you may have scouted agents, paid your way to writing conferences, and/or relentlessly queried publishing companies until you landed a publishing deal. Or you went the indie route and did all of the proof–editing, cover design, and layout yourself, or you paid to have it done freelance.

Regardless of how you got here, you are now the author of a published book. If you are a new author, you may have been led to believe the hard work is over, that you can sit back, kick up your feet, and wait for those royalty payments to roll in. I hate to be the bearer of bad news, but now that you have a published book to your name, it is your job—not your publisher's or your writing group's or your mother's—to make sure your book reaches as many potential readers as possible.

If you are like most writers, your advertising budget either does not exist or suffers from very finite limitations. Wouldn't it be nice to find an almost boundless source of websites that would be willing to advertise your book for free? Welcome to the world of blog tours, where you can shell out a few free review copies, and maybe a prize or giveaway now and then, in exchange for promotion to thousands of readers in your niche market.

What is a Blog Tour?

It used to be that authors who wanted to promote their books would go on a book-signing tour—stopping at bookstores, libraries, etc. with a trunk full of hardcover books just waiting to be sold. In a world where brick and mortar bookstores are floundering and readers are flocking to eBooks instead of print, authors are moving away from the traditional book tours in favor of blog tours (sometimes also known as virtual book tours). Individual blogs take the place of bookstores, libraries, and other physical locations where authors used to stop. Readers interact with authors in forums and comments instead of in book-signing lines. Authors do not take massive time away from their writing and everyday lives, nor do they have to pay hefty transportation expenses or hotel fees.

Unless you have seen one done, the idea of a blog tour might still sound a little daunting. Although there are several kinds of blog tours, they all share these two things in common:

1. **Blog tours need blogs.**

    The most common blog tours are set up so that a book is featured on a different blog each day. Usually, these blogs are book review sites dedicated to reviewing books in a certain genre. In addition to promoting the book, each blog might share a blurb or graphic. They might also include a link that you can click on to find all the other posts in the same blog tour.

2. **Blog tours last a specific amount of time.**

    Some blog tours are short, reaching just three or four blogs in a few days. Others can last longer, as long as there are enough participating blogs. A blog tour, however, has a definite start date and a definite end date. If you give away twenty-five review copies of your book to various bloggers and ask them to post a review at their convenience, you may be featured on several blogs and gain exposure for your book, but you have not set up an actual blog tour.

This book is written for authors, both traditional and self-published, who want to increase their exposure through blog tours. If setting up an actual tour sounds a little too daunting, nearly all of the information presented here can be applied to approaching individual blogs with requests for reviews. You don't have to do it large-scale, but if you want to, this book will show you how.

Why Should I Bother?

You are a writer. You want to spend your time writing. I get that. I really do. But if you just plan to write twelve hours a day and never lift a finger (or click a button) to market and promote your books, you are probably missing out on the sales you could enjoy with a little more effort.

To have a successfully marketed book, you don't just need a catchy cover and a carefully edited manuscript. You need publicity. You need people to *talk* about your book. Think about the books you see for sale in the check-out line at the grocery store. Which one are you most likely to pick up: the one you have never heard of, or the one you have seen spotlighted on talk shows, advertised in magazines, and recommended by several of your friends?

Publicity—getting your book (and its cover) in the public eye—is crucial to good book marketing. But you don't want people just to know about your book and recognize it by its front cover design. After all, some books gain notoriety because their writing is so bad or their message is so offensive. While some might argue that there is no such thing as bad publicity, I think most of us would agree that, given the choice, we would like our books to come with high recommendations. That is why reviews are so important, whether they come from Amazon customers, book-review bloggers, or your next-door neighbor.

Engaging with a number of bloggers provides you with publicity and reviews, both of which are vital for book marketing success. By showing up on various blogs, your book title, its cover, and your name are getting free exposure. Some blogs have upwards of a thousand follow-ers. Even if only a third of those see the post about your particular book, that is still hundreds of readers who otherwise might never have heard of you or your writing. If you show up on multiple blogs, readers have a chance to see your book cover more than once. Some experts state that the average customer sees a book's cover seven times before actually buying it. Repeat exposure in this case can only be a good thing for your book and its message.

In addition to the increased publicity that comes from getting spot-lighted on various blogs, you will also get reviews. It is hard to come up with a single more important factor to a book's success than posi-tive reviews. Think about the most recent movie you went to see in the theater. Did you go because you heard great feedback about it? Would you have wasted your money on tickets if everyone you talked to said it was terrible? Although there is no guarantee that the blog-gers who feature your book will give it a positive review, the chance to get people of influence recommending your book to their blog fol-lowers is too good of a deal to pass up, especially since you are not paying the reviewer anything except for a free copy of your book.

Participating in a blog tour provides you with a lot of publicity on a variety of blogs, all within a short period of time. Hopefully, the ma-jority of these reviewers will give you high recommendations to their readers. The increased exposure and chance for positive reviews are reason enough to get involved in a blog tour. There are also a few additional benefits to blog tours worth mentioning:

1. **Increased reviews on other venues.**

   If a blogger takes the time to review your book on their blog, he or she will often leave a review at places like Amazon and Goodreads. Even if they don't do this automatically, most reviewers will respond positively to a polite request to post their reviews on Amazon after they feature you on their blogs.

2. **Growing relationships with book reviewers.**

   Not all bloggers are going to turn into your best friends, but you might make a few connections that carry on past the blog tour. In addition to finding fun people to interact with, you might find these bloggers are a great first-source to turn to when you get ready to publish another book or want help promoting a special deal.

3. **Connecting with readers.**

   With all the technology available to us today, most of us authors don't just sit behind our desks and type all day. We are "out there," even if only in the virtual sense, connecting with readers and potential readers. When a blog posts a review or spotlight of your book and people comment, you can go back and interact with these readers in a way that is much more personal than hacking out one-sided tweets or spamming book forums online.

4. **Search engine optimization.**

   If someone wants more information about you or your book, there is a decent chance they will google you or look you up in another search engine. Imagine someone typing in your name or the name of your book and getting hit with dozens of links to reviewers talking about your work. You will definitely come across as more professional than the author whose name only comes up with a personal blog or author webpage.

5. **Viralability.**

It's great when your former college roommate tells you she loves your book, but, unless she is telling everybody else how much she loves it as well, her feedback is only going to boost your ego, not your sales or visibility. With blog reviews, you (and anybody else) can share a reviewer's feedback with an ever-growing audience of social networking friends and fans, who may in turn either buy your book or pass the review on to others.

6. **Blogger commitment.**

I have already mentioned that you can take nearly all the information in this book and apply it as you approach blogs one by one. If you send your book to a blogger to review and don't have a blog tour, however, you never really know when that reviewer is going to review your book. Having definitive days you are asking bloggers to commit to can help ensure your book does not get stuck at the bottom of a reviewer's ever-growing to-be-read pile.

7. **Increased social media following.**

    If you have a giveaway in connection with your blog tour, you can expect to see an increase in Twitter followers and Facebook fans (more on this in Part Two). Your fan base is a great asset when it comes to launching your next book or approaching a potential agent or publisher.

As I've said before, setting up a blog tour may take a decent amount of work, but the increase in visibility and the potential for direct sales, coupled with all the side benefits mentioned above, can bring exponential rewards.

CHAPTER TWO

Types of Blog Tours

In this section, we will talk about 7 different types of blog posts you will see on blog tours. Please keep in mind that many authors will incorporate several of the following aspects into one blog tour. For example, you don't have to have a blog tour of *just* author interviews, but you may ask a handful of bloggers to join your blog tour by offering interviews, while other bloggers might do reviews or spotlights. There are almost as many blog tour types as there are genres of books. The kind of blog tour you set up can be as unique as the book you are promoting.

Reviews

What it is: A review post is a post where a blogger leaves a review of your writing. Most will also include a cover image, a brief synopsis of your book, and links so readers can purchase it. Some bloggers have a star system to rate the books they read.

Reviews are probably the most common type of a blog post to be found on a blog tour. If you are scheduling a blog tour, you will want to make sure to have a decent number of bloggers who will actually review your book. Most authors are already keenly aware of the many benefits of reviews, so we will just touch on them briefly. Positive reviews lend credence to your book. Many people won't read a book they know nothing about; they rely on reviews.

Blog reviews can be even more influential than Amazon reviews. When a blogger reviews your book, they are essentially recommending your writing to all of their followers (assuming the review is positive). As we already mentioned, many bloggers will also include their reviews on Amazon, Goodreads, and other important review sites.

What it looks like: For an example of simple book review posts, you can see my post on Cristi's Reviews at: www.trainingauthors.com/blogreview-example. This is a book review coupled with a giveaway that was part of a blog tour I put together for one of my novels.

Note: You can learn more about the benefits of book reviews, and other ways to get reviews, in the first book in this series, "How to Get Honest Reviews."

Cover Reveals

What it is: A cover reveal is one of the easiest kinds of blog posts. The name is just as it suggests; a cover reveal post on a blog is meant to show off your cover to a wide range of readers to create buzz (or pre-buzz) for your book.

Your cover is the stamp of your book. It is the way your readers and potential readers will instantly and visually connect with you and your writing. Obviously, you want to make sure you have a gripping cover that stands out well even as a thumbnail image. Once you have nailed down your cover (or received your cover image from your publisher), the next thing you want to do is make sure people see it. Remember, the average reader will see a book cover at least seven times before purchasing it.

You can schedule a cover reveal even before your book is published. By including an image of your book cover and a short blurb or excerpt, you can get people excited about your work before it is even released. A cover reveal blog post can include links to preorder your book or to sign up for your mailing list to be notified when the book is ready to purchase. Be careful, however, that you don't let too much time lapse between a cover reveal and your publication dates, or else people will forget about your book and you will lose any momentum you gained. You also need to make sure that the cover is totally ready to reveal. Just think how embarrassing it could be if you ask a dozen bloggers to post your cover, and then you, or your publisher, decide to change the title or the cover image.

Cover reveals do not have to occur before your book is published. If a blogger does not have time to read and review your entire book, a cover reveal is a simple way for her to tell her readers about what you have written and include links to purchase the book.

Remember, even if people don't buy your book directly, they still have that mental image of your cover branded into their minds. If they see the cover on Amazon or someone else's blog in the future, they may be more apt to purchase it.

What it looks like: For an example of a cover reveal, you can see this post from Elaine Jeremiah, an author friend of mine who participated in one of my blog tours by posting an image of my novel's cover: www.trainingauthors.com/coverreveal-example.

First-Chapter Reveals

What it is: This type of post involves a blogger posting (or "revealing") the first chapter of your book to his readers. The idea is to gain enough interest in your writing that people will then go and buy your book.

Most authors today know readers should be hooked well before the end of the first chapter. Many experts even recommend hooking your reader with the very first paragraph, or even sentence. In other words, your first words should leave your readers dying to purchase your book so they can keep reading. A first-chapter reveal can be a great way to hook potential readers this way.

First-chapter reveals do not have to be anything fancy. You can just send the blogger your first chapter. Make sure it is well-edited, of course. Blog readers don't necessarily like to read thousands of words, either, and so if your first chapter goes way over the 1k word count, consider just including the first few pages. If you end at a scene's climax, you will be more likely to hook some readers.

What it looks like: This post from A Book Lover's Retreat will show you what a typical first-chapter reveal looks like: www.trainingauthors.com/chapterreveal-example.

Guest Posts

What it is: A guest post is something you write that the blogger includes on their blog and attributes it to you. It is like a professor who hands one lecture over to a traveling specialist.

If bloggers ask you to write a guest post, it is always nice to at least ask if they have any topic suggestions. Be expected, however, for them to tell you to "write whatever you want." In that case, it is best to spend a little bit of time on each blogger's website so you can get a feel for what kind of audience they cater to. You would not want to write a guest post about the wonderful vegan lifestyle on a website geared toward hunters. Unless it is related to your book, you should probably avoid politics and controversial topics completely. Don't be too lengthy, either. Most people don't care to read more than eight hundred words on a blog post.

Guest posts are a great chance to be creative. If you write historical fiction, consider posting recipes that fit the era you write in. If you are a self-help writer, giving out free advice is a great way to promote your book. Just remember, as a guest blogger, you should act like a guest. Don't make every other sentence a hard sell for your book, or you may never get invited back!

What it looks like: Guest post topics can vary greatly. For example, during my very first book blog tour, I wrote one guest post about a typical day in my life (www.trainingauthors.com/aterry-guestpost1)and later wrote a guest post for another blog about religious persecution, one of the more serious themes in my novels (www.trainingauthors.com/aterry-guestpost2).

Author Interviews

What it is: In an author interview, the author answers questions about her writing and/or life. Readers like to know about their favorite authors. Participating in author interviews can be a great way to engage your present fans and find some new ones.

If someone offers to host an author interview with you, they may send you a list of questions or they may ask you to come up with your own questions and answers. Some bloggers get really funky and creative with the type of questions they ask (*What was your weirdest dream ever and what does it say about you as a person?*), while others stick to the basics (*Why did you write this book?*).

Some bloggers will give you just one round of questions; others will ask a few questions, wait for your responses, and then ask a few more. Good etiquette means replying to interview questions in a timely manner. Try not to let more than four or five days go by without sending off your responses. Author interviews are a great place to let your personality shine. Be polite and respectful, and try to talk about things besides just your book.

If you find yourself involved in several author interviews and you are asked the same or similar questions on several of them, consider including your most common responses in one document that you can use as a cut-and-paste template to save time.

What it looks like: This post gives you an example of a very typical author interview: www.trainingauthors.com/aterry-interview1, while this interview from Regi McClain shows how zany some interviews can get: www.trainingauthors.com/aterry-interview2.

Character Interviews

What it is: Some blogs and fiction authors get really creative and set up character interviews. As the name suggests, these are interviews between the blogger and one of your fictitious characters.

The process of creating a character interview is basically the same as that for author interviews above. The difference is that your character will be answering the questions, not you. The blogger is also more likely to have read your book already so he can ask appropriate questions.

Character interviews are by nature less formal and more spontaneous than some of the more standard author interviews. It is not a time to hold back, unless your character is ridiculously reserved. Think of what makes your character unique and reveal that to your readers. It doesn't have to be the protagonist who gets interviewed, either. Some great character interviews have come from minor characters (especially those who might feel jealous that the protagonist gets so much attention) or even the villain.

What it looks like: You can see an example of a character interview on this blog: www.trainingauthors.com/characterinterview-example.

Book Spotlights

Some bloggers won't have time to read your book or come up with interview questions. If they still want to participate in your blog tour, they may offer to do a book spotlight, which is the quickest and easiest type of blog tour post.

What it is: A book spotlight has nothing but the basics: your name, the name of your book, a cover image, purchase links, and a short blurb. In this way, it is similar to a cover reveal, but many times it will be the author, not the blogger, who comes up with *all* the content for a book spotlight post.

What it looks like: When my first audiobook came out, I contacted several bloggers who had already reviewed my book and asked them to do a spotlight announcing the audio release. I sent them the entire post ahead of time, and it ended up looking like this post here: www.trainingauthors.com/spotlight-example.

There are two ways to set up a spotlight post. You can either send the blogger all the information mentioned above and let them put it together in a post, or you can send it to them ready to go. One way to do this is to create in a Word document what the post would look like. As I already said, book spotlights are very basic. Include the information listed above, save the document, and send it to your blogger.

If you have some blogging experience on your own, you can even send bloggers the html code so all they have to do is copy it and paste it into their blog. This kind of pre-fabricated post is probably the easiest post for bloggers to put online.

[*Note: Skip the following section if you have limited experience with blogs and/or html codes.*]

To create a pre-fab post, go to your own blog and create the book spotlight, including links and images, as you would want it to appear on someone else's blog. If you are in Blogger or WordPress, there is a simple button you can click to turn that post into html code. All you need to do is copy this code and email it to your reviewer. Be careful, however, as some things like giveaway links may not work when converted from one blog platform (like Blogger) to another (like Word-Press). I don't recommend doing this unless your post is very basic (text, images, and links only) or you have quite a bit of experience with html coding. Remember, you can always send the information, pictures, link, and text to the bloggers and let them format it themselves.

In the Mind of Bloggers

If you are going to set up a blog tour, you are going to spend a decent amount of your time interacting with bloggers. With this in mind, it is helpful to get a feel for what makes bloggers tick. Remember, book review bloggers can be some of your biggest fans and most important marketing assistants.

If you only learn one thing about bloggers, it should be this: Bloggers want traffic. They want people to visit their blogs. This will not be the only time I mention it in this book, either. Blog traffic is currency to bloggers. Blogs with high enough traffic will show up high in search engine results. In this way, blog traffic leads to more blog traffic, which leads to a happy blogger.

Some bloggers blog because they love to read. Getting free review books from authors is reason enough to do what they do. Many bloggers also monetize their blogs, meaning they actually earn money from their websites. Most bloggers are set up as Amazon affiliates, for example. When someone buys a book off their website, they (the blogger) get a small commission from Amazon. Blogs with high enough traffic can earn a decent amount by affiliate sales alone (which is one reason why bloggers love traffic).

If a blog has a large enough following, it can also earn money in direct advertising fees. Imagine you are a blogger who reviews fantasy fiction. Your blog has such a high following and gets so much traffic that authors are willing to pay you to include an ad in the sidebar of your blog.

One important point to mention is that book reviewers are never paid for *reviewing* a book. Paid advertising only refers to links in the sidebar (clickable images, not reviews). Paying a blogger for a review is never an acceptable practice, and any blogger who accepts money in exchange for reviews is acting unethically.

Speaking of ethics, you should never offer bloggers anything in exchange for a review except for a free copy of your book, but you can help out bloggers in many ways, like promoting their posts to give them more traffic or signing up to publically follow their blogs.

Are You Really Ready?

Like most things worth doing, blog tours take a decent amount of work to set up and facilitate. There's nothing like rushing in to something enthusiastically only to find out it was a lot more of a time or energy commitment than you expected. Here are some important questions to ask yourself before you jump on the blog tour bandwagon:

1. **Is my book ready to send to multiple reviewers?**

    Asking your exercise buddy or great-aunt Bertha to read your book is one thing. It is quite another to send it to bloggers you do not know who agree to leave honest reviews, even if those reviews are far from stellar. (Note: You should *never* ask a reviewer to only post a positive review. You will come across as immature, self-centered, and unethical.) Before engaging in a blog tour, make sure your book is well-edited and fits the highest standards of your genre. Remember, the bloggers you are approaching are usually very well-read individuals who hold to very high professional standards of writing and editing. If your book is not ready for that kind of market yet, get it ready!

2. Can I handle negative reviews?

When you send a book to a reviewer, there is no guarantee you will get a positive review back. While most authors recognize the need to develop thick outer shells, most of us still crave acceptance and accolades. If you do not feel you could handle strangers potentially picking your book apart paragraph by paragraph, a blog tour might not be for you.

3. Can I afford to give out review copies?

Bloggers receive the books they feature on their blog for free. If you are planning a blog tour with upwards of twenty blog stops, the price tag of mailing paperbacks will quickly add up. Thankfully, many bloggers accept eBook copies of review books. Some blogs, however, still require paperbacks, and you need to include these expenses in your budget. If you are traditionally published, you need to check with your publisher to see if you will be expected to buy and mail these review copies. Some publishers will send review copies for free to a certain number of individuals. Others will expect you to do so yourself at your own expense.

4. Are there enough blogs in my niche/genre?

If you write fiction, this probably won't be a problem at all. You can find book reviewers who review just about any genre imaginable. If you write nonfiction, especially if you write in abstract fields with small followings, you might want to do some research ahead of time and see if there are enough blogs about your subject of expertise to warrant a blog tour. Remember, you can use almost all of the principles in this book to get yourself featured on just one or two blogs as opposed to engaging in an actual multi-blog tour.

5.   Do I have the time to put into a blog tour?

Blog tours are a lot of work to pull off. The more blogs that host your book, the more work you need to put in. All this effort takes time away from your other commitments. Are you at a point in your personal life and writing career where you can make your blog tour run smoothly? Can you see yourself investing time in querying bloggers, scheduling posts, sending review books, answering interview questions, commenting on blog posts, etc. for the next several weeks/months?

Now that you've gotten familiar with the concept of a blog tour, if you decide to promote your book in this way, it's time to decide whether or not you will plan the entire thing yourself or hire a service to help you out. The following chapter details the pros and cons of both options.

CHAPTER THREE

Do It Yourself,
or Hire a Service

If you hate communicating by e-mail, don't know a single blogger, or possess the organizational skills of a toddler, you might want to look into paid services that set up your blog tour for you. These professionals will find you bloggers, schedule posts, and generally ensure your blog tour runs smoothly.

The Pros

There are many benefits to hiring a blog tour service, some obvious and some more subtle.

1. **Organization.**

   Blog tour professionals are a tremendous asset to individuals with poor organizational abilities. If the thought of maintaining a calendar with a dozen or more different blog posts sounds daunting, you might consider a paid service.

2. **Networking.**

   Paid blog tour services are also a nice option if you do not know many bloggers or feel like it might be hard to find reviewers in your particular genre. Simply put, blog tour professionals know more bloggers than you do. Blog tour services can help increase your network of blogging acquaintances. Some authors using a paid service for their first blog tour, maintain relationships with the bloggers they meet, and do their own blog tours for subsequent releases.

3. **Legitimacy.**

   If you are published independently or through a small press, you may experience some of the snobbiness that still gets directed at self-published authors. Some reviewers don't accept queries from indie authors, especially if they are reviewers with large blog followings and lots of solicitations for reviews. Sometimes, however, these individuals will respond more favorably to a book offered through a blog tour service than they would if you were to approach them yourself.

4. **Open Doors.**

   A good blog tour service will connect you with bloggers you otherwise could not reach. Some reviewers do not publish their contact information. Instead of getting bombarded with review requests, these bloggers prefer to hand-pick which books they look at, and they hear about these books a lot of the time through blog tour services. For this reason, hiring a reputable blog tour service can open doors you could not enter on your own. It is important to note that it is usually the large blogs, with upwards of a thousand followers, that have the luxury of being more choosy about their review books and don't publicize their contact information or accept reviews directly from authors.

5.   **Increased Participation.**

If you set up a blog tour yourself and get 25 different bloggers who agree to "host a stop" (i.e., post about your book on a particular day), let's just guess that about half will do so automatically. Another ten will post their review once you send them a polite reminder email a few days before their scheduled post. And a few will not do it at all. When you are the author, there is not a whole lot you can do to *make* a blogger fulfill her commitment. Blog tour services, however, because they are not directly invested in your book and because they are a business organization, see closer to 100% participation in the blog tours they schedule. If a blogger wants to continue getting free books from the blog tour service, they need to fulfill their commitments or risk getting booted out of the review program. This is a considerable incentive for the bloggers to get their posts up on their scheduled days, but if they are just dealing with the author, there is no guarantee they will get to their post in time.

The Cons

Although there are several benefits of hiring a blog tour service, there are also several potential draw-backs.

1. **Cost.**

   The most obvious deterrent to hiring a blog tour service is the money involved. Some authors spend eight or nine hundred dollars to throw a huge blog tour for their debut novel that only results in a couple dozen books sales. The economics involved in paying for a high-end blog tour service may not be realistic for every author.

2. **Less Relationship.**

   When you pay for a service, you will be dealing mostly with the blog tour organizer, not the bloggers themselves. They will tell you which blogs need guest posts, for example, and in many cases, you will send the documents to the blog tour service, not the bloggers. This method is probably more efficient but results in less interaction (and therefore less relationship) with the bloggers involved.

3. **Less Control.**

   When you sit back and let someone else choose which blogs will host stops on your tour, you really don't get much say in the matter. If you have strong political views, for example, your book still may appear on a blog with a vastly different philosophy than yours. People who see your name associated with that blog might just assume you are connected by more than just a paid service. Perhaps you write wholesome teen fiction that promotes strong moral values, but one of the stops the blog service schedules for you is on a catch-all book review site that also promotes hard-core erotica. For some people, this is not a problem. For others, it can be unsettling.

4. **(Potentially) More Busywork.**

Another point worth considering is that even if you hire a service, you will still be responsible for all your author interviews and guest posts. Some blog tour services tend to utilize these quite a bit for "filler days" (or days that they could not find an actual reviewer for the schedule). It is possible that by paying someone to set up a tour for you, you will end up committing to more interviews and guest posts than you otherwise would have.

Third Option

Some services will help schedule posts and send reminders on your behalf, but you are the one who contacts bloggers. This is a nice option for individuals who already know a decent number of bloggers but could use an extra hand on the organizational side of things. This type of tour usually costs quite a bit less, as well, since you will be the one initiating contact with potential reviewers. It also ensures you maintain a higher degree of control than you would if you went with a full-service company.

My Personal Experience.

My first experience with blog tours was with a paid service. The top benefit wasn't in sales but in an increase in amazon reviews (which I desperately needed at the time). I ended up on over forty blogs. Many of these, however, were just guest posts or interviews on catch-all fiction sites. I learned from my experience to seek out sites more specific to my target audience.

I didn't earn back the money I spent on the blog tour, at least not during the course of the tour itself. I also had no idea going into it how much time I'd spent on mailing books, answering interviews, and writing guest posts. However, I do consider the tour eventually was worth the time and money. I met a lot of bloggers, many of whom have featured me on their blogs three or four or even more times. One of the bloggers also nominated my book for an award that I eventually won, and that *did* lead to an increase in sales right away.

Since I didn't recoup my initial investment in sales, I never paid for a blog tour service after that first time, but I created several blog tours on my own. These tours, I'm happy to say, resulted in much more direct sales increase, probably since I was targeting blogs only in my genre. I also focused a lot more on review posts and not the filler posts.

My most successful blog tour was coupled with a 99-cent sale of one of my novels. For my giveaway, I offered free copies of my novel to the first three people from each blog who left a comment. In this way,

I helped out the bloggers (by giving their readers a reason to comment). I also had a nice giveaway (leading to increased traffic) that didn't cost me a whole lot of money. The reason I limited the prize to the first three people who commented was so that anyone else who wanted the book but didn't get there soon enough could then go and purchase it. This blog tour, coupled with a few other paid promotional services, resulted in my novel reaching #1 in three different amazon lists. (You can see one of the posts and how the giveaway worked at: www.trainingauthors.com/giveaway-example.)

I probably won't pay for a blog tour service again unless I switch genres and need some help finding a new community of bloggers. Setting up the blog tours on my own, however, is quite time-consuming. I do value the contact I have with my blogging friends, however, and don't want to give that up.

What to Look for in a Service.

If you are going to be paying someone to plan, schedule, promote, and implement your blog tour, you want to make sure to hire only the best. You certainly do not want to pay a chunk of cash to someone who will slap up a few guest posts, plan a few author interviews, and rack up your writer debt. Here are some questions to ask yourself before you hire a professional for your blog tour.

1. **Do they have a good track record in my genre?**

    Look at the blog tours they have already done. If all the books they promote are historical fiction and sweet romances, they might not be the best fit for your vampire horror piece.

2. **Do they include a nice mix of interviews, guest posts, and other fillers <u>as well as actual reviews</u>?**

   At least a third or more of your blog tour posts should probably be reviews of your book. Half would be even better. Check out your potential service's history. Is their ratio of filler posts to review posts skewed? (*Note:* Some services offer review-only blog tours. These are nice options for no-frills authors who do not really care about investing time answering questions about their favorite childhood pet or writing half a dozen guest posts. On the other hand, a review-only tour will probably be smaller and perhaps more expensive since it is more commitment on behalf of the bloggers involved.)

3. **Do their bloggers have a following?**

   Before you hire a blog tour service, I suggest picking a book they have recently promoted that is similar in genre to yours. Go to the blogs that participated in that tour, and check out how many followers they have. Most blogs have lists in the sidebar that give you an idea of how many subscribers, Twitter fans, Facebook likes, etc. that particular blog boasts. There is no real break-down here, but a small blog might have less than one hundred followers, and a large blog closer to a thousand. Although it is not realistic to only show up on blogs with five-hundred followers or more, you do want to make sure that your potential service has at least a handful of medium and large blogs in their database. Avoid blog tour services that only utilize blogs with a dozen followers or so; it is not going to be worth your time *or* money.

Wrapping It Up.

There are many good reasons authors choose to hire a blog tour service. In the next section, we will talk about how to set up your own blog tour. Once you see what is involved, you may end up considering the professionals. On the other hand, even if you are paying for a service to set up your blog tour, you will still be responsible for things like answering interview questions and mailing review copies. I suggest you still at least browse through the next section, as a lot of the steps involved will apply to you as well.

Blog tours are time-intensive endeavors, and a blog tour service can take some of the stress off. You may find this a nice way to gain publicity and stay sane, or you may decide to keep your money for more important things (like groceries!) and do it all yourself. The next section will tell you how.

PART TWO

Do It Yourself Blog Tours

This section will help you with all the steps to set up your own blog tour. Even if you have already decided to pay a professional blog tour service to run your blog tour on your behalf, you should still read the last two sections (*During the Tour* and *After the Tour*), because these are things you should do whether someone else has planned the tour for you or not.

CHAPTER FOUR

Before the Tour

You will want to plan your blog tour at least four to eight weeks in advance, perhaps even more if it's going to be a larger tour. As you'll find out in this chapter, there are several steps to take care of even before your blog tour starts. The more organized you are during this step of the process, the smoother your blog tour is likely to run.

Choose Your Blogs

If you are connected with any author communities, your author friends who maintain personal blogs sound like the logical first choice to turn to when looking for blog tour hosts. In general, authors are great at promoting other authors. Keep in mind that if you are asking a lot of other colleagues to review your book on their blogs, you should be willing to return the favor for them in the future.

While your author community is a nice launching point, you should try to get your book reviewed by bloggers in other fields as well. If you write fiction, search for book review blogs in your particular genre. (The most comprehensive list I've found that breaks down bloggers by genre is found at www.theindieview.com/indie-reviewers/.)

If you write nonfiction, you may also want to find blogging experts in your niche market. For example, if you write humorous memoirs about your experience as a home-schooling mother in a large family, you could search for some of the most popular mommy blogs or homeschool blogs and approach them about doing a review.

When searching for bloggers, Google will only take you so far. Also, Google searches are designed to show the most popular blogs first. Bloggers with high ranks on Google may be too busy to review your book in a timely manner. Thankfully, there are many other ways to find review blogs. If you are on Facebook, consider joining a few groups for bloggers and/or writers in your genre. There are numerous Facebook groups dedicated just to connecting writers and reviewers. Try searching Facebook for "author" and "reviewers" or "authors" and "bloggers" and see what comes up. You can also narrow your search by genre. Many bloggers also keep a "blog roll" in their sidebar. This is a collection of links to other blogs that these bloggers follow. If you write fantasy and notice a blog roll on a fantasy review site, chances are that many of the blogs listed there also review books like yours.

You can also see which blogs participated in blog tours for writers in your same genre. If you write suspense and see that another suspense author has participated in a blog tour, you can see what other blogs reviewed or spotlighted her book. These could be a good bloggers for you to approach as well.

Bloggers often go to great lengths to constantly increase their readership. You can see how many followers of blog has by noting how many subscribers are listed in the sidebar. Obviously, blogs with higher readership numbers will lead to increased publicity for you and your book. If you are mailing paperback copies to reviewers, you might want to query the larger blogs first.

You might also decide to give free electronic copies of your book to smaller blogs, while offering paperback copies to blogs with a large enough following. (*Note:* Some authors *only* offer electronic copies to reviewers, regardless of blog size. This is entirely your prerogative. Be careful to read each blog's review policies first, however, since some only accept paperbacks.)

Keep Records

If you plan to arrange your own blog tour, you need to keep very careful records. Organizational skills are a high priority. When you are doing your initial research to find blogs that fit your niche market, design a spreadsheet and keep it updated. At the very least, you should include the name of the blog, the URL, and the permalink to the blog's review policies. You should also record the name and email address of the blogger if you can find this information on their blog. If you want to be extremely thorough, keep notes about what kind of books each blog likes to review and whether or not they accept paperback, eBook, and/or both. This information is usually found in the blog's review policies.

To add a personal touch, you might make individualized notes to include with your initial query for each blog. If you come across a blog that reviews books but also has dozens of pictures of the blogger's prize-winning pit bulls, make a note to comment on how cute his dogs are in your first email. This is not necessary, but it sure beats sending the exact same form letter to dozens of bloggers.

Read the Review Policies

Before you approach bloggers to request reviews, it is very important that you read their review policies very carefully. First, you need to find out if they are accepting reviews and if they read books in your particular genre. You will also find contact information (some prefer email, some prefer contact forms) and whether or not they review eBooks or paperback books. A few blogs do not read books by self-published authors. Others keep their blogs entirely family-friendly and do not want any books with highly sexualized or violent covers or themes. Following the rules spelled out in the review policy shows professionalism and respect for the time the blogger puts into their website.

Some blogs do not have review policies. In these cases, it is okay to send them an email about your book to see if they want to review it. But if there are review policies posted on the blog *you must read them!* Of course, in addition to reading the review policies, you need to follow the blogger's guidelines to a tee. If a blogger says, *We don't review romance or historical fiction*, do not waste time by sending them five paragraphs trying to convince them to review your book set during the Civil War about a girl from the North who falls in love with a Confederate soldier.

Query the Reviewer

Reviewers are like agents and publishing companies—they don't want unsolicited manuscripts. Before you send a copy of your writing to a potential reviewer, send them a polite e-mail or contact them directly via their web page contact form. (If you search a blog and cannot find an email address listed anywhere, chances are the reviewer does not want to be contacted by authors directly. Move on to another blog.)

In your initial email, tell the reviewer about your book. Remember, the reviewer is doing you a favor, not the other way around. You need to pitch your book with the same fervor you would use pitching an agent or acquisitions editor. Do not make up lies, but be sure to put your book in the best light possible. Do you have a large number of four- and five-star reviews already on Amazon? Tell them! Have you won awards for previous books in the past? Mention it!

Reviewers have better things to do than read pages and pages of queries. Keep your note simple. Give your pitch, but keep it to a sentence or two. Include the short form of your book blurb (not a synopsis) and be sure to spell out the genre. It might be helpful to include a link to your book's listing on Amazon or an image of the cover to help catch a blogger's eye. Keep this section to a short paragraph.

If you want the blogger to review your book, this is all you have to do. If you want the blogger to actually join a blog tour, you need to give this information up front. Have the dates of your blog tour already set. This will help the reviewer determine if he has time to read your book and post his review in time. Ideally, you should query a reviewer at least six to twelve weeks before your blog tour starts. If your blog tour will include a giveaway, mention this in your query. Blog posts with giveaways give the blogger more traffic than standalone blog posts. If you are interested in including things like author interviews, cover reveals, or book spotlights as well as just reviews, this is a good time to mention it. If the blogger is too busy to read and review your book, he still may be willing to give you a little publicity in the form of a cover reveal or spotlight, especially if there is a giveaway involved.

I used something similar to this standard query when I first approached bloggers about reviewing one of my suspense novels:

Dear _____,

I am looking for bloggers interested in joining a blog tour for my next release, *Slave Again*, an inspirational suspense novel set in East Asia. The protagonist in *Slave Again* escapes a North Korean prison camp and is trafficked across the border into China. The blog tour will run from [dates], and I will be offering a $50 gift-card giveaway designed to increase traffic to your site.

Please let me know if you would like a review copy of *Slave Again*. I have paperback and electronic copies available for review. If you're not able to complete the review by the blog tour, I could also send you information for a spotlight post.

Send Out Review Copies

Once you have queried the reviewers, they will let you know if they are interested in receiving a free review copy. It probably does not need to be said, but I will go ahead and say it anyway: A book reviewer should never have to pay for your book. If you mail a paperback copy, you pay for both the book and the shipping. If the reviewer asks you for a copy of your book to give away on her blog, she is asking you to do so for free. It is understood from the beginning any books you send the reviewer will be sent freely, even if she ends up unable to post a review on her blog.

Once you have heard back from a reviewer and he/she has requested a copy of your book, it is even more important to keep good records. First, you need to ask your reviewer what format they want to read your book in. If they want a paperback copy, you need to collect their mailing address and mail the book promptly. If the blog tour is only a few weeks away, do not risk sending your book media rate just to save a few bucks. Most reviewers invest hours a day into their blogs, and many do so without any direct compensation. Have respect for their time, and mail your book as soon as possible. If you include a personal note, you can thank them for taking the time to read your work.

As soon as you mail a book out to a reviewer, make a note in your database so you can keep track of who has received review copies and who has not. If your book is an advanced review copy (ARC, sent out for publicity purposes before it is actually published), you should include a note in the book itself stating that this copy is an ARC. Readers will be much more tolerant of typos and small grammar errors in an ARC than in a published copy.

Some bloggers will offer to give your book away on their blog after they have read it. As I already mentioned, blog posts with giveaways will get more visits than blog posts with no incentives involved. However, some authors feel like people are less likely to purchase a book if they have just entered a contest to win it for free. I personally like to ask reviewers to wait at least two weeks from the date of their initial review before they offer the book as a giveaway. This also serves the purpose of double exposure. There is an initial post with the review, and second follow-up post with information about the giveaway. Remember, the more people see and/or hear about your book, the more likely they will be to buy it.

It is important to understand, however, that when you mail a paperback copy of a book to a reviewer, it becomes their property. They might sell it. They might give it away on their blog. They might donate it to their local library. They might burn it. Whatever they do with it is out of your control. The best you can do is include a polite note when you send the book, asking that they refrain from including it as a giveaway until after your blog tour has ended. And never be so tacky that you ask a reviewer to return your book to you when they are done.

Many reviewers prefer receiving electronic copies, which is great news for us authors. Electronic copies cost absolutely nothing. The two most common ways to send electronic copies are by sending a PDF or an EPUB attachment to an email. You can create a PDF directly from a Word document by downloading free software like Pri-moPDF or PDF995. You can also google search programs that will let you upload a Word document online and have it converted to EPUB. (Note: If your book contains fancy formatting, some of your formatting may be lost in this process.)

If PDF or EPUB does not work for you or your reviewer, there are other options, too. If your book is up on Smashwords, you can send your reviewer a download coupon. This requires a little more work from the reviewer, and it is not quite as easy as an email attachment, but most reviewers will be familiar with using Smashword codes.

You could also send a reviewer a gift copy of your book if it is published on Kindle. To do this, go to your eBook's sales page on Amazon and click the tab on the side that says *Give as a gift*. There are pros and cons to this option you will want to carefully consider. The most obvious deterrent is that you actually have to pay to send gift copies. While it is fine to do this every once in a while, you may not want to make this your default method for sending review copies. You should be careful to only do this with reputable reviewers, too, since if they wanted to, they could take your gifted eBook and exchange it for an Amazon gift card.

On the plus side, you do get some of your money back from royalties, and the sale will also count toward your book's rank (assuming the reviewer actually accepts the gift from Amazon). You should be sure to ask your reviewer to include the required statement that they received your book for free in exchange for an honest review, however. Some people have trouble with amazon pulling down reviews of gifted copies that don't include the disclaimer. It will be up to you as the author to determine whether or not you'll use Amazon gifted copies with some of your reviewers.

I *don't* recommend getting a bunch of reviewers lined up, setting your book for free, and then asking them to download it. This comes across as tacky and offensive. Remember, the bloggers are doing you a favor by reviewing your book. Ethically, the only gift you can give them in return is a free copy of your book. If your book is already free, you are basically asking them to work for you for absolutely nothing.

Schedule Posts

By the time you contact potential bloggers about your book, you should have the dates of your blog tour set. Typically, smaller blog tours last a week. Larger ones can run a few weeks. A blog tour that lasts a month or more has the potential of becoming very hard to manage logistically. I recommend only doing a long tour if you are using a paid blog tour service that will help with some of your organizing or if you have already conducted smaller blog tours before and know what to expect.

After they commit to reviewing your book, most bloggers will want to sign up for a specific date. Bloggers can schedule their reviews in advance, so if they know the date ahead of time, they can have most or all of the work done before it is time for their post to go live. Scheduling posts is probably the most time-consuming and trickiest part of your blog tour. Thankfully, there are online tools that can help you.

If your blog tour is small, with bloggers you mostly know already, you can probably just ask each blogger what day they prefer to post their review. If you are only scheduling five posts for a five-day blog tour, this isn't too tricky. It just involves a few emails back and forth and a calendar either on your desk or online.

If you would like to go bigger with your blog tour, however, I highly recommend using an online signup form. This will make things a lot easier for you as well as the bloggers you are working with. With an online schedule form, bloggers can see which days are available and choose what fits their schedule. Some bloggers, for example, do not blog on weekends, or they only post things on certain days of the week. With an online signup form, the bloggers can see which days are available and then sign up for the day they want.

In the past, I have used www.signupgenius.com, which is a free service and is fairly easy to navigate. As an added bonus, you can configure your settings so that the website sends emails to everybody who signs up for a blog post a few days in advance to give them a friendly reminder.

Set Up Your Giveaway (Optional)

Imagine you are on Facebook, and you see a link to a review by someone you barely know who is talking about a book you have never heard of. Are you likely to click that link? No.

Now, imagine you are on Facebook, and you see a link that says, "Book Review ~ Enter to Win a $100 Gift Card!" Will you go there now? The chances just increased, didn't they?

Hosting a giveaway as part of your blog tour can increase traffic exponentially. Giveaways work kind of like a raffle, but instead of buying tickets, people earn entries. You can earn entries by doing things like following somebody on Twitter or liking their author page. You can also earn entries by sharing the contest link or commenting on a blog post. A book review post with a contest has a lot more chance to go viral than a post without a contest, since a lot of the people who want to win will share about the contest to earn more entries.

In addition to increasing traffic, running a giveaway can give you a real boost in followers, fans, and subscribers. My first blog tour with a paid service stretched on for several months, but I didn't run a giveaway and didn't get any new Facebook followers. On the other hand, I've run a week-long blog tour that has led to over fifty new Facebook fans and several dozen newsletter subscribers when coupled with the right kind of giveaway.

Another perk of giveaways is that bloggers might be more willing to join your blog tour if a giveaway is involved. Traffic is to bloggers what Amazon rankings are to authors. In other words, a blog's success is judged by the number of visitors it gets. Bloggers know a giveaway, especially a large giveaway, will lead to a lot of hits, likes, and shares. By including a giveaway, you are helping out the bloggers involved in your book tour, and you may get some interest from bloggers who otherwise might not want to join.

As I have already mentioned, hosting a giveaway is not necessary for a blog tour, but it does increase traffic to each post, giving you more publicity and your bloggers more hits. If you do decide to set up a giveaway, there are several websites that help you set it up.

Rafflecopter historically has been the most popular choice to running giveaways. It is easy to use, and once your giveaway is set up, it will give you a link you can share with your blog tour hosts where they can run the exact same giveaway on their blogs. Punchtab and Wildfire are other sites that help run giveaways.

Setting up a giveaway is a several-step process. First, you need to decide on a prize. Including a free copy of your book may sound like a good idea, but remember a blog reader who just entered a contest to win your book for free now has a lot less incentive to go out and buy it. The chances of that reader coming back to the blog two weeks later to see if a winner has been chosen, and then going to Amazon to buy your book, is pretty low.

Some authors do include giveaways of their book, and the choice is certainly up to you. If you are running a blog tour before your book is published, this could be a nice way to earn some pre-buzz for your upcoming release. If you have several books already published, you could offer a gift basket with your other writing as a nice prize to a lucky winner. Remember to state clearly whether your giveaway is open internationally (like if it is an eBook or gift card you can send the winner online) or not. That way, you won't get stuck paying the bill to mail a prize to a foreign country.

The two most common kinds of prizes to win from these kind of give-aways tend to be gift cards (Amazon is a hot choice, mostly since people reading review blogs tend to buy a lot of books) and eReaders (for the same reason). These are both good incentives to get people to click on the blog post and enter the contest. And remember, everybody who clicks on the post, even if it is just to enter the contest, has seen a cover of your book. They might not buy it that day, but if they see it again in the future (or again and again and again), you may end up with a new fan.

Speaking of fans, some authors come up with cute book-related paraphernalia to use as prizes for giveaways. Bookmarks, coffee mugs, and key chains that are personalized with your book cover or title can be fairly cheap giveaway prizes that are easy to order (I recommend vistaprint.com) and not too large to mail. If you are an author with a large following, these could be awesome prizes for your fans. On the other hand, if nobody knows who you are and they have not yet read your book, getting a brand-new pen in the mail with your author tagline might not be all that exhilarating of an experience.

Fiction writers can have a lot of fun creating gift baskets that are pertinent to their novel. If you write cozy mysteries set in the tropics, you could create a gift basket with all kinds of beach-related trinkets, or even practical things like sunscreen and sunglasses. Just remember that you will be responsible for shipping, which can significantly bump up your budget if you are not careful.

If you write nonfiction, consider offering a free service as a giveaway. I once entered a giveaway on a site that promoted books for authors, and I won a free four-page critique by an author I already followed and whose writing craft books really helped me tighten my writing style.

Remember, your giveaway prize should be something you can afford and something readers will appreciate. Once you have chosen your prize, you will also need to come up with the ways that readers will earn entry points. Here are a few pointers as you decide what to include for entries:

1. **Keep it simple.**

   Most people get annoyed with giveaways that have dozens of Facebook pages to like or Twitter accounts to follow. Stick to just two or three accounts, and you won't get things too complicated.

2. **Don't make them leave the blog.**

   It's great to have people sign up for your newsletter, for example, but don't include external links in your giveaway. Giveaways should be short and simple to enter. I like to include an entry that just says, "Click this box to be added to my newsletter." Then, when I see the entries at the end of a giveaway, I can add them to my mailing list. This makes a lot more sense than telling the entrants to click an external link, sign up for your email list, open their own email account, confirm that they want to subscribe to my email list, then go back to the original giveaway and prove to me they have signed up.

3. **Don't make them buy something.**

   As soon as someone has to pay to enter your giveaway, that giveaway becomes a lottery. Lotteries are governed by about a gazillion state and federal rules that none of us authors have time to research and abide by. It might sound tempting to make someone buy your book to get entered in your giveaway, but it is not necessarily legal.

4. **Include perks for your bloggers.**

   Bloggers want to get something out of your giveaway, too. Consider leaving a few entries to benefit your blogger, like leaving a blog comment, following a blog, or liking the blogger's Facebook page.

Once you have your giveaway set up, you need to find a way to get the information so your bloggers can include the giveaway on their own blogs. Do not just give them a link to the giveaway on your website, for example. Giveaways work best when they are embedded into the blog you are visiting, not when you have to click a series of links just to get there. Most of the giveaway services include a link or a copyable html code you can give to the bloggers so they can include the giveaway on their blogs.

Prepare Your Publicity Packet

As soon as you can, you should send your reviewers the publicity packet they will need to do their posts. This is true whether the bloggers are reviewing your book or participating in your blog tour in the form of author interviews, book spotlights, etc.

Once you have prepared your publicity packets, send them to your bloggers as an attachment or online file they can access *as soon as the materials are ready*. Remember, many bloggers like to work ahead and have their posts set up ahead of time so they don't have to worry about it.

The following should be included in every publicity packet:

- **Your book's cover image**.

  Include this either as an attachment, or provide your bloggers with a website where they can access the photo online.

- **Your (short) synopsis**.

  Blog readers don't necessarily read every single word of a blog post. Keep your synopsis short and sweet, maybe three or four sentences max.

- **Your author bio and photo**.

  Not all bloggers will include this information on their posts, but it is nice to send out to those who do want it.

- **Your links**.

  Include links to purchase your books, as well as links to your website and social media pages.

- **A blog tour graphic (optional)**.

  Many authors include their own blog tour graphic. This graphic is usually rectangular and appears at the bottom of a post. It should have your name, your book's cover, and the dates of your blog tour. The text usually says "[Title] Blog Tour." You can make this graphic yourself, hire it out to a freelance designer, or skip this part all together. You can visit the following website to see an example of a blog tour graphic: www.trainingauthors.com/tourgraphic-example.

- **Your giveaway information (optional)**.

    If you are planning a giveaway in conjunction with your blog tour, make sure you let your bloggers know how to run the giveaway from their website. If your giveaway is through Rafflecopter, there is a link you can give bloggers so they can include the giveaway on their sites as well.

Finish Your Guest Posts and Author Interviews

Some authors set up blog tours that only feature reviews. Unfortunately, not all bloggers have time to review every book they receive queries about. If a blogger does not have time to review your book but offers you a guest post, author interview, cover reveal, or book spotlight, I would go for it. Reviews are great, but any medium that gets your name, your book's title, and its cover in the public eye—especially if the exposure is free—is worth taking.

When you set up your blog tour (or if you have someone set it up for you), you will probably schedule at least a few posts like these. It is very important that you get the information your bloggers want as soon as possible. Yes, I am sure you have better things to do than answer mundane questions about your book, but that is what blog tours are all about. Just make the best of it and approach it with a genuine and respectful attitude. Remember, author interviews are a great way for your readers and potential readers to learn more about you as a person. Give thoughtful, concise answers, and try to have fun. There's nothing wrong with recycling answers, either, if several bloggers ask you the same question.

During the course of your blog tour, you may also end up writing some guest posts. Writing for someone else's blog can be daunting. You basically have a blank screen and a general feel for the kind of blog you will appear on. Researching other guest posts on that same blog can help give you a few ideas. No matter what you end up writing about, make sure it is well-edited and polished, keep it less than 800 words (as a general rule), and send it to your blog host in a timely manner.

Create a Hub Site (optional)

It is nice to include one place that lists all the stops on your blog tour. If you have a small blog tour, your blogging friends will appreciate having their websites posted. If you are setting up a large, extensive blog tour, it is also a nice way to keep track of which bloggers have featured your work. Then, when you get ready to publish another work, you can approach the same people.

Although it is not essential to have a hub site for a blog tour, it definitely adds a degree of professionalism to what you do. Usually, you can set the hub site up through your own personal web page. You can give it a name like: www.YourWebsite.com/blogtour. Include your graphic if you are using one and make a list of all the blogs that will be participating in your tour. Hyperlink your list of blog posts so when fans click on each blog name, they will be taken to that blog. Remember, blog hits are gold for bloggers.

An added benefit of having a hub site is you can promote it during your blog tour in addition to promoting the individual blogs that feature your work. When I paid for my first blog tour service, they created a hub site for me—you can visit it at: www.trainingauthors.com/hubsite-example.

Send Reminders

A week or so your before your blog tour begins, you should send a reminder to the individual bloggers who are going to participate in your blog tour. In addition to thanking them for taking the time to promote your book, you should ask them if they need any more information from you. Even if you have already sent out your publicity packet, a few bloggers might have missed it. You should also remind each blogger what day they signed up for on your tour.

If you are managing a lot of bloggers, you can use the same form letter for each, changing just the name and the date of their scheduled post. Remember to be courteous and let the bloggers know how much you appreciate the time they have put into your book.

Now that you have found your bloggers, prepared your materials, and scheduled your posts, your blog tour should be good to go. Keep a close watch over your email for any last-minute questions your bloggers might have, and then don't go on vacation just yet. There is quite a bit of work to do while your blog tour is running, as well.

CHAPTER FIVE

During the Tour

With the scheduling over and out of the way, and your guest posts and author interviews all taken care of, the bulk of the work is behind you. Now, it is time to interact, publicize, and try to have some fun.

Remember, bloggers love traffic to their blog. They also love comments. A blog with a lot of comments will get higher ranks in Google's algorithm and give the blog more publicity. During the time of your blog tour, your goal should be to see lots of traffic and lots of comments on the blogs participating in your tour.

Leave Comments

First of all, it is polite to leave a public comment on each blog that features you during your tour. This is when organization comes in so handy. If you have a list of all the blogs, the URL address, and the dates of your blog tour stops, stopping by each blog should only take a few short minutes a day.

As you comment on each blog post on your tour, leave a brief thank-you. Personalize it if you can. For example, if the blogger shares that they read your book on vacation, tell them you are glad they got to get away for a little while. If others have already commented on the blog, it is polite (but not necessary) to leave comments back for them, too. Just remember, this is a forum, not a sales call. Don't be pushy about buying your book, simply tell them you are glad they stopped by.

At this point in your tour, you may come across a few bloggers who did not care for your book. Thank them for taking the time to read it. Doing this on a public forum, like their blog, can show others that you are a polite, reasonable individual who can handle criticism. Just like with nasty Amazon reviewers or internet trolls, I do not recommend getting into any debates. Keep it simple like, *Thank you so much for your feedback. I'll keep it in mind for my future books.* Do not feel like you need to defend yourself. Remember, it is your writing—not you—they did not like, and that could have been for a myriad of reasons.

The only time I would recommend defending yourself at all is if you sent the reviewer an ARC (advanced review copy), told them it was an ARC, and they still complained about typos. A quick note can show the public that the comments were based on an advanced copy and that issue has been addressed. (*Thanks so much for your review. Sorry the ARC was frustrating for you to read. Thankfully, the book has gone through professional editing and the mistakes should be cleared up now.*)

Similarly, if a reader (or troll) leaves a comment that is nasty or rude, it is probably best to ignore it. Getting into a debate with an unreasonable troll is not the best use of your time and may not lead to many PR points.

Share and Tweet

You should do something to publicize each blog that hosts a stop on your blog tour. One of the easiest ways to do this is to click one of the social media icons on the blog post itself. If you have the blogger's handle or account name, tag them so they can see you promoted them. This can go far in creating a strong, mutually-beneficial relationship between you and bloggers.

Your shares and tweets don't have to be anything profound. You can say something like, "Thank you, [blogger's name], for your kind review of [book title]," and then include the link so anyone who sees the post can click and go to the original post.

Another common way to promote review posts is to share a short sentence or two from the review: "Check out [blogger's name]'s review of [book title]: [include short quote and link.]"

If you have a prize associated with your blog tour, you can encourage people to go and enter the giveaway: "See [blogger's name] review of [book title] and sign up to win [gift card, free book, etc.]"

If you want to go the extra mile, sign up to follow the blogs that featured you. Increased followers means increased rankings for blogs. Remember, if you help out bloggers today, they will be more likely to feature you tomorrow (or whenever you are ready with your next release, free-day promo, etc.).

Say Thanks

It is not necessary, but sending a personal email thanking each blogger involved in your tour can be a nice gesture. If you plan to write more books in the future, you may also wish to ask the bloggers if they would like to review other books later on. Be sure to keep track of those who say yes. (Remember to keep that database updated!)

No-Shows

Like I already mentioned, the average blog tour (especially the do-it-yourself kind) will probably have a few no-shows. Someone who signed up to host a stop will have failed to do so by the date they committed to. When this happens, you have two choices. You can either ignore it and count it an expected "loss," or you can send the blogger a polite email to see if she wants to post on a different day. Do not make your note accusatory, but offer to reschedule her post if she would like and let her know you would still love for her to join the blog tour if at all possible.

Whether or not you do this is up to you and your own personality. Some authors prefer to take one missed blog post over a potentially awkward exchange. On the other hand, sometimes bloggers simply forget or realize last minute they were missing links, etc. they needed for their post and are glad to be sent a reminder.

Keep Up Your Hub Site

If you have created a hub site where you list permalinks to all the blogs who participated in your blog tour, you should update it each day as you get links to blogs that featured your book. This will also come in helpful in the future if you ever need a reminder of where you've been hosted before.

Check Stats

This section is definitely optional, but if you keep a note of your book sales or book rank each day of the tour, it can give you a feel for a few things, like (1) if your tour is generating any immediate increased sales and (2) if certain blogs lead to greater sales than others. These would definitely be blogs you would want to mark on your database to communicate with again if you ever plan another blog tour.

Remember, blog tours are about publicity as much as direct sales. Ideally, your blog tour will lead to some direct sales (customers who click a link on the blog and buy your book right then). If you have high praise coming from high-traffic blogs, you can expect a decent amount of impulse purchases. Even if you don't make hundreds of sales during your blog tour, do not be discouraged. Remember, readers tend to see a book half a dozen times or more before they actually buy it. The long-term returns from your blog tour will likely outweigh the immediate return of direct sales, even if you do see a significant increase in numbers.

CHAPTER SIX

After the Tour

When your scheduled blog tour is over, the hard part is now behind you. There are, however, a few small matters of business to take care of before you move on to another project altogether.

Giveaway

First of all, you need to take care of whatever prizes you offered during your giveaway (if you ran one). Rafflecopter, or whatever site you used to host your giveaway, will choose random winners for you. If for some reason you find that you need to choose random winners some other way (for example, if you promised a prize to one blog commenter), you can use www.random.org, a website that will generate a random number between any two numbers you enter.

Send your giveaway prize in an efficient and timely manner. It is always nice to include a note congratulating the winner. If your prize is a book, signing your autograph adds a nice personal touch. Many people also congratulate the winner publically on Facebook or Twitter. In addition to making sure the winner hears that he/she won, you also are informing the other entrants that (1) you *did* award a prize, and (2) it did not go to them.

Database

You may have noticed a theme going on here; keeping up your blogger database is valuable for future marketing. Even if you never run another blog tour, you still may want bloggers to help pitch in every now and then by announcing one of your free promo days to their readers, etc. At the end of your tour, make a note of all the bloggers who fulfilled their commitments, and also mark any no-shows. You may also choose to include permalink to their specific blog post, as well as note what kind of post it was (review, interview, and so on).

More Thanks

If your bloggers have not heard you thank them at least five or six times by now for participating in your blog tour, you should do it again! Remember, bloggers can be an author's new best friend.

Conclusion

I hope by now you see how a blog tour can increase publicity for your book, give you a boost in immediate sales, get you in touch with bloggers who can help you promote books in the future, and help you interact with potential readers you could have never found on your own. You have probably also come to realize that blog tours are a lot of work in addition to being a great marketing tool. Whether you decide to hire a blog tour service, set up a tour on your own, or just use the information to approach bloggers one by one, I would like to personally wish you the best of luck as you continue on in your writing career. I look forward to seeing you and your books in the blogosphere sometime in the future!

To your success,
A. Terry

P.S. As you know, reviews are gold to authors. If you have found this book helpful, would you consider leaving an honest review on Amazon.com?

ABOUT THE AUTHOR

A. Terry

A. Terry's books have been featured on over a hundred different book review blogs and mommy blogs over the past year. She writes inspirational suspense and children's fiction and has received several awards for her writing.

ABOUT THE PUBLISHER

Shelley Hitz

Shelley Hitz is an award-winning and internationally best-selling author. She is the owner of TrainingAuthors.com and is passionate about helping authors succeed in publishing and marketing their books.

And she teaches from personal experience. Shelley has been writing and publishing books since 2008 and has published over 30 books including print, eBook and audio book formats.

Connect with Training Authors Online

Access Their FREE Author Training Here:
www.TrainingAuthors.com/Newsletter

See A Complete List Of Their Books For Authors Here:
www.TrainingAuthors.com/Books

Connect with Them on Social Media:
www.facebook.com/trainingauthors
www.twitter.com/trainingauthors
www.youtube.com/trainingauthors

OTHER BOOKS IN THE
BOOK MARKETING SURVIVAL GUIDE SERIES

Ranging from topics from how to run a book launch, to networking, to offline marketing, this series has something for every author--no matter what stage of the book marketing journey you're in. Each survival guide has a matching toolkit available where authors can access templates, checklists, video tutorials and more on the topic covered in the book.

Volume 1: How to Get Honest Reviews

Offering credibility and proof of readership, reviews have the power to boost your book sales. In this book, we'll share multiple ways that authors can legitimately increase the number of reviews written about their books.

Get the book here:
www.trainingauthors.com/books/honest-reviews

Get the corresponding toolkit here:
 www.trainingauthors.com/courses/reviews-kit

You can find the rest of the books in the Survival Guide Series on our website at: www.trainingauthors.com/survivalguides

ADDITIONAL RESOURCES

Training Courses

Access our database of templates, trainings and more with our training courses for authors. Find out more here:

www.trainingauthors.com/courses

Our Books for Authors

We have an entire library of books for authors, including books on publishing and marketing. Check out the entire list here:

www.trainingauthors.com/books

Recommended Outsourcers for Authors

If you need help with the technical side of publishing and marketing your books, consider outsourcing to one of our recommended providers here:

www.trainingauthors.com/recommended-outsourcers-for-authors

Tools and Resources We Use and Recommend

Check out the tools we use and recommend for writing, publishing and marketing here:

www.trainingauthors.com/resources

22520091R10051

Made in the USA
Middletown, DE
01 August 2015